Yara

My Friend from Syria

By Alhan Rahimi

Illustrations by Anahit Aleksanyan

To find out about other books by the author, visit the "Children's Books" section on

www.persianarabic.com

or email

alhan@persianarabic.com

Dedicated to

Every child who had to endure hardships!

It was Monday morning and Oliver was in his classroom, concentrating on the new grammar lesson being explained by his teacher, Mrs. Smith. Suddenly, there was a knock on the door. It was Mr. Maxwell, the principal of the school, who entered the classroom with a girl walking behind him. She seemed shy.

As they stood by the door, Mr. Maxwell whispered something to Mrs. Smith. She, then, smiled and made way for Mr. Maxwell to move forward and talk to the class. Mrs. Smith took the girl's hand gently and walked her over to her desk.

"This is Yara, our new student," said Mr. Maxwell. "She arrived in Canada just two days ago. Although she could have started school next week, she was eager to start earlier. Please help her with any lessons she missed and make her feel welcome in her new home."

Yara was wondering what her new principal was saying. She knew he was talking about her, but did not understand the details of what he was saying.

"I would also like you to know that Yara speaks three languages. She is a native Arabic speaker, fluent in French, and has some basic knowledge of English. I am sure she will be fluent in English in no time at all. It is your responsibility as her classmates to help her improve her English. Does anyone have any questions?" No one raised their hand. Everyone was stunned into silence!

All the students were wondering where Yara had been prior to coming to Canada. Angela was one of them. She remembered what her parents were saying a few days ago about Syrian families coming to Canada. "Maybe she's from Syria!" she thought. She was very impatient to go to Yara's desk and talk to her, but class wasn't over yet. Still, something seemed strange. Yara was not looking at them!

Oliver was wondering the same thing and was eager to learn more. "Maybe Yara feels shy" was a thought that crossed Oliver's mind. "After all, everything must be new to her. A new school, new classmates, new classroom, new teachers, new language, new house and a new COUNTRY!" Oliver thought, as he was looking at Yara. "She's smiling, but I am sure she misses her friends back home. I will try to become her friend."

When it was break time, Oliver and Angela were the first to rush towards Yara. They smiled at each other, nodding.

Oliver opened his lunch box and offered Yara his apple. "Hi, Yara! Would you like to have an apple?" he asked.

Yara looked at the apple, then looked at Oliver and shook her head. Her lip started to quiver.

"What's wrong?" Oliver asked.

Yara covered her face and burst into tears.
Oliver and Angela were perplexed.

"Why are you crying, Yara?" asked Angela. Yara kept her face covered, sobbing softly.

Angela and Oliver didn't know what to do. While they talked, Yara was in another world. Her thoughts were back home. Looking at that apple brought back so many memories.

She remembered Syria and the apple tree in their front yard. She had many beautiful memories there of how, every day, her parents had their afternoon Turkish coffee under its shade, while she and her siblings did their homework beside them on their picnic mat.

On the weekends, she and the children of their neighborhood would hold hands around the apple tree and dance their traditional "dabke" dance. Sometimes, the parents would join them. They all loved singing and dancing together.

Once, when Yara and her friends were studying under the tree, something funny happened. They were reading about Newton's discovery of gravity when, suddenly, an apple fell on one friend's head! Everyone started laughing at the silly coincidence. They started calling him 'Isaac Newton'. It made him feel flattered. Those were good times.

Yara also remembered the saddest night in her life.

While Yara held her bunny warm in bed, her father woke her, and also her sister and brothers, in the middle of the night and told them they had to leave immediately. At that moment, Yara didn't understand why but, later, she would find out that war had started in her country and it was not safe to be there anymore. They had to leave quickly and her mother could prepare only two suitcases for the whole family.

"Mama, I want to take my storybooks," Yara said.

"We cannot take them, sweetheart. We don't have enough space for anything more," her mother replied.

"What about my bunny, Mama?" she whispered, about to cry. "I have to take it."

Her mother looked at her, took a deep breath, and gave her a big hug. "Okay, you can take your bunny with you."

But that was it. All she could take from her bedroom was that one bunny and the few clothes her mother packed. Yara had to leave everything else behind... everything.

A friend of her father came to pick them up that very night. But as they were sitting in the car, Yara asked her father for one more minute. He agreed, but he told her to hurry.

It was slightly windy and chilly as she ran to the apple tree and hugged it with her tiny arms. She kissed its trunk and looked up at its beautiful branches. "I will miss you, our beautiful apple tree," she said. "I am sorry that we have to leave you here alone. I promise to try my best to come back to you one day. Please watch over our house and allow the other children to come and play under your beautiful branches." Then, she bent over to the ground and took a few of its fallen leaves with her.

"Hurry up, Yara! We have to leave now!" cried her father. She rushed back to the car but, as they left, she viewed the apple tree from the window, until it was out of sight. She placed the leaves in a little box and decided to keep them with her all the time. It was a little piece of home that she could take with her.

While Yara cried, remembering her home, Angela and Oliver were worrying and discussing what could have made her cry.

"Was it something I said?" asked Oliver sadly.

"No, Oliver, I heard you. You were very polite!" replied Angela.

Yara wiped her tears, looked up at her two classmates and knew they were only trying to help her. "One moment," she said, putting on a smile.

She reached into her bag and took out a box. She carefully opened it and showed it to them. "Look!" she said. "I love apples."

Oliver and Angela looked inside. They were surprised by what was inside the box! All they could see were a few cracked and dried leaves. Those leaves must have been important, but they didn't understand what they meant. Maybe Yara could explain it to them when her English improved.

Still, they were happy she showed them. All that mattered was that she was smiling again.

Yara was excited to have new friends with who she would be able to share her memories... one day!

Dear young reader,

Hope you enjoyed this book. If you have any thought, opinion or comment about this book; please, share them on the review page on Amazon.

Also, if you have suggestions for other books that discuss important issues happening in the world, I would love to hear from you. I will try my best to include them in my coming books. Send me an email on alhan@persianarabic.com.

Love,

Alhan

Made in the USA
Middletown, DE
06 January 2017